Relativity

Also by Kelly Cherry

Sick and Full of Burning, a novel

Lovers and Agnostics, poems

Relativity

A Point of View

Poems by KELLY CHERRY

LOUISIANA STATE UNIVERSITY PRESS

BATON ROUGE 1977

Designer: Albert Crochet
Type face: VIP Caledonia
Typesetter: Graphic World
Printer and Binder: Kingsport Press, Inc., Kingsport, Tennessee

Some of the poems in this collection have previously
appeared in the following publications, to which grateful
acknowledgment is made: *Appalachian Journal, Aspen
Leaves, Dacotah Territory, Four Quarters, Greenfield
Review, Greensboro Review, Inland Writers Magazine,
Lyric, Plume and Sword, Remington Review, SMART:
Readings in Science and Art* (Red Clay Books, 1975),
The Sou'wester, and *Three Rivers Poetry Journal.*

Lines from Book I of *De Rerum Natura* from *Lucretius:
On the Nature of Things,* translated by Palmer Bovie.

LIBRARY OF CONGRESS CATALOGING IN PUBLICATION DATA

Cherry, Kelly.
    Relativity: a point of view.

    I. Title.
PS3553.H357R4   811'.5'4   76-45643
ISBN 0-8071-0276-8
ISBN 0-8071-0277-6 pbk.

For my parents

Contents

IV

V

Some are bearded
& walk falling forward
into bright, thin air;
some wear something borrowed

or blue; a few
dance on Saturday night,
splaying the space around them
with limbs of light

that tease the shadows
from the wall:
These are my poems,
my people—

I

Good night, ladies, good night, sweet
ladies, good night, good night.

—T. S. Eliot (after Shakespeare)

Lt. Col. Valentina Vladimirovna Tereshkova

first woman to orbit the earth,
June 16–June 19, 1963

It looked like an apple
or a Christmas orange:
I wanted to eat it.
I could taste the juice
trickling down my throat,
my tongue smarted,
my teeth were chilled.
How sweet those mountains seemed,
how cool and tangy, the Daugava!

What scrawl of history
had sent me so far from home? . . .

When I was a girl in school, comrades,
seemingly lazy as a lizard
sprawled on a rock in Tashkent,
I dreamed of conquest.
My hands tugged at my arms,
I caught flies on my tongue.

Now my soul's as hushed as the Steppes on a winter night;
snow drifts in my brain, something
shifts, sinks, subsides inside,

and some undying pulse hoists my body
like a flag, and sends me up,
like Nureyev.
From my samovar I fill my cup with air,
and it overflows.
Who knows who scatters the bright cloud?

Two days and almost twenty-three hours
I looked at light,
scanning its lines like a book.

My conclusions:

At last I saw the way
time turns,
like a key in a lock,

and night becomes day,
and sun burns away the primeval mist,
and day is, and is not.

Listen, earthmen,
comrades of the soil,
I saw the Black Sea shrink to a drop
of dew and disappear;
I could blot out Mother Russia with my thumb in thin air;
the whole world was nearly not there.

It looked like an apple
or a Christmas orange:
I wanted to eat it.
I thought, It is pleasant to the eyes,
good for food,
and eating it would make men and women wise.

I could taste the juice
trickling down my throat,
my tongue smarted,
my teeth were chilled.
How sweet those mountains seemed,
how cool and tangy, the Daugava!

A Riddle

My beauty is beyond compare
And easy reach. No man would dare
To comb my loosed, effulgent hair.
I keep my distance but on rare
Occasions condescend to bear
Eight things that move a man to prayer
(Yet none's a child), then disappear
In broad daylight beyond blue air.
Man's grasp still falls just short of there.

Answer

A comet. *Coma* means hair. According to a verse published
in the seventeenth century, the comet was thought to bring
"wind, famine, plague, death to kings, war, earthquake,
floods, and direful change."

Earth

My eyes are empty basins of the sea.
I have relinquished all my tears to light
and air: the metal of my heart's rusty
as a spar abandoned along the site
of drought, a desert in the Thorax Plain!
Every hope has died; the carcasses
are strewn upon the sand where sun has slain
them, bleached to geologic pallor, as is
the way with those women whose looks will turn
a man to stone or self to salt. What Lot
is mine? I lie alone at night and burn
by day, and even when I'm cold I'm hot
and wild, and yet my womb's a wasteland, bare
of love. No future will survive long there.

Dora

said old
dead things
with her hands,
wings

of
    rough birds
that turn harsh
as words
when you look at

them
    plainly:
Dora's death
is a dull retort
in a short

hard and grained
cold dead
verse of visible
birds of lead.

Curie

Radium is my element.
My complexion has taken on the warm glow
of an experimental tint.

My hands display
chemical burns, nails
broken like brittle kindling. The X-ray

is another name for my eyes.
Shield yourself or let them show you
how far below the surface beauty lies

like a molten core, magmatic rock bed
from which a spark is sometimes struck
turning lava into lead,

my poor philosopher's stone.
A modest miracle, but one
admirable in woman.

Jezebel

Like a bitch, I bury
My bones in the moist soil,

Digging halfway to hell.
Roots and white bulbs burn

In the aerated earth, fiery
Genesis shooting sparks

Upward along slender stalks
To flame into full flower

The red rose bed.
My marrow bleeds

A rising course similar to this:
Redemption sheds its bright petals

On the far-reaching wind,
While I discover myself

Everywhere, in all the elements,
Alive despite aspersion

And the wages of sin, in nature
Forgiven.

Joan

The fire has tongues
They lick at my limbs

My breasts are being consumed by sweet heat
How they smoke and melt

My little hell is man-made

I will relinquish my chaste ghost
To the murmurings of these fiery mouths

And turn and turn in the sulphuric spit!

But body remains, like the aftertaste
Of love, and all my ashes cling

To the throat and won't go down

The Melancholy Muse

I hate it. This waiting.
This balancing on the edge of things to come.
The slow transit of the sun across my sheet.

At noon I grind the heat between my legs.
At three I think of young men, poets, and Stephen Crane,
His excess flesh burned away by the pretty fevers of his brain

Saving only cool light, shining eyes,
To show me that my warm surprise had a use for some.
I'm no one,

A voice without sound, stray moon
Void of reflection, movement
Without direction, untouched,
A woman without wings

Grounded in the past which every man has fled, leaving me
To love alone, at the last, in the dark, among the dead.

Self-Portrait

Old elbow,
you feel like lemon peel

My mind is rind

I am a still life
scattered over gleaming cloth
subtly shadowed, tart
textures oozing out of an informal frame

My arteries are art! pump a pert
juice, that fey trickle in the far corner,

drawing flies

II

Perhaps it was right to dissemble your love,
But—why did you kick me downstairs?

—John Philip Kemble

Transformations

I

You cast me out
and up: I spin and drift,
slow as Argo in the southern skies.
Old-power, sweet-dream, only-one,
I remember your world—

Green and blue, continents
the color of shale, whole
seas gritty with salt, air
transparent as quartz!

I remember your hand on my back
like the shell on a snail,
and ground-shadows blown by a cloud-rack.

II

Look at this: The celestial equator
emits tropical light waves.
I burn and blink.

I compass your planet
like the sun in Ptolemy's time,
burning, blinking.

III

Heat is energy in transit
but it's a one-way street,
hot to cold, and I'll never get to meet
you coming. This, though I can say hello in Greek and Sanskrit!
You pass me by.
I'm as insignificant to you as the sky.

Be warned: An ice age is dawning.
Scintillating ice crystals are forming
secretly at the edges of things—of Vermont, Maine,
the Antarctic Ocean.
Heat is in motion.
I am becoming rain.

IV

Old ever-real, nothing's
true: Space flirts with time
and time cheats on you.
She says she's going shopping—
in that negligee? She leaves you in the lurch.

Only I remain, devious
as Democritus, assuming
atomic weight, spending
passion in the process.

I feel my way slowly, in the dark, underground,
and surface at your grave
like an artesian spring, and all the past is drowned.

The Tent

I'll tell you how it was: as silent as your own reflection, you squatted,
sharpening your spear's point on a flint.
The sun came up over your left shoulder.
When you stood and walked, the grass burned your soles—
you hopped and howled, and I lay down at your feet
like a pet.

The wind wrapped itself around my waist like a thong, knotted
loosely. I wondered what your moodiness meant.
The day was becoming darker and colder.
You kept watch by the outer rocks, digging holes
for our hides and meat,
to keep them safe, and our vegetables, to keep them wet

and fresh. At dawn, buffalo dotted
the horizon, and flowers filled the air with wild scent.
You turned toward me and saw I was growing older,
like the earth. Then, solemnly, out of dried skins and some pine poles,
you fashioned a tent where the two of us would meet.
How could you forget?

The Doorway to Doom for Objects

"For in whatever part you say the atoms
First begin to fail, this part will be
The doorway to Doom for objects . . . "
—Lucretius, *De Rerum Natura*

It opens in the heart,
Today and tomorrow.
First love must depart,
Then sorrow.

And then the rest of the world
Says thank you and good-bye,
Crossing the threshold
To die.

A whirlwind sucks all things
Like liquid through a straw.
The great door swings
Wide, the great maw

Swallows all energy
And soon nothing will stay.
Moral entropy
Cuts short the play

And ends the party too.
We go out to go in.
We go into
Nothing, or Sin.

And There Is Freedom of a Kind
Even in Mere Magnitude

I shall praise his bulk,
the cave of his chest
in which I have my rest

while wearisome worries skulk
like outlaws along the perimeter
of the bed where my feet are

protected by the sheer hulk
of him. No anxiety can scale
this mountain of a male

or find me out when I flee
to sexual sanctuary!
Safe by virtue of his arms,
I set aside the old alarms
(my feminine charms).

Sequence Sonnet

I will bring bouquets to his house,
Volumes of verse and Beethoven's Ninth,
Seventh, Fifth, Third and Eighth.
Gaining confidence, I will compose
Sonnets on the subject of masculine beauty
As a direct function of time.
When his face has become a mockery
Of the one I fell for, I will tame
My laughter like a savage cat
Washing itself on the high cliff.
In our passage from love to the last, wild, selfish grief
Which knows nothing, I will conduct
This gentle man through the garden of courtship.
Civilization is a sweet though short trip.

Translation: After Petronius Arbiter

To His Uncoy Mistress

I warn you, dearest, such delight
leads only to a dark despair.
And are we beasts of burden then,
to trample blindly, dumbly there?

A thing that's done is soon forgotten.
Such success is misbegotten.

But with a little grace and wit,
we'll make a brighter race of it,
and idly kissing, come to pass
all brutish souls who come too fast. . . .

(And in such sexual evolution, through our night's eternity,
overturning nature, will I please you, and you, please God,
please me!)

A Dialogue Between Mars and Venus

FIRST SPEAKER

The two attendant moons, Fear and Dread,
float face up in your "canals" like bloated fish, reflected.
I dredge them up like old boots,
wave arms and bluster as you will.
I catch; I don't kill.
Now why are you turning red?
See here, General, that high color is a warning signal,
to watch your heart.

SECOND SPEAKER

I would watch yours.
You hide your heart
beneath thick clouds—
your rock heart.
Oh yes, the astronomer loves the hours
he lives in Palomar's dome.
You are his one home,
and mine.

III

When a Man has Married a Wife, he finds out whether
Her knees & elbows are only glewed together.

—William Blake

My Marriage

(Genus: *Lepidodendron*)

It goes under like a spongy log,
soaking up silica.

I love these stony roots
planted in time, these stigmaria,

this scaly graduate
of the school of hard knocks,

these leaf-scarred rocks
like little diamonds.

And the rings! . . . the rings
and cells that show forth

clearly, fixed and candid
as the star in the north.

Giant dragonflies, corals,
the tiny bug-eyed trilobite

grace this paleosite
with shell and wing, cool,

amberstruck exoskeleton,
nice flash of improbability

felled and stuck, past
petrified in present, free

from possibility's hard and arbitrary
demands. Once, seed ferns swooned,

languid as the currents in a lost lagoon,
while warm winds swarmed over the damp earth

like locusts, and rain was manna.
I hold that time still.

Divorce keeps it real and intact,
like a fossil.

The Housecleaning

I am mistress of my own mind,
caretaker of the cranium

In the spring
I brainclean

(Only a man might mistake
this chore for brainwashing)

I wash the windows to my soul

Straightening out the chinks,
discarding,
letting the light shine in,

I sweep the useless & the uninvited
from view, show the door
to you

& you & you—
my memories of thoughtless men

I Will Cut Out My Heart

I will cut out my heart
It has tricked me into desire
Betrayed its body and myself
Been a liar

I will cut out my heart
It has urged me to hope
Leapt like spring and stolen
The end of my rope

For this one last time
I will cut out my heart
It has bound me to love
And pulled me apart

As Between Wisdom and Youth

As between wisdom and youth,
Choose beauty every time.
It was loss that taught me this:
Prose will not rhyme
Nor art own up to truth,
The real to the sublime.
When the stars begin to fall
Choose beauty every time.

She Remembers the Tears

She remembers the tears
the sun drew from her
on a hot day, the way
panic strikes and sears
the soul, a small puff
of smoke, but enough

so it disappears:
a smudge of ash
on a round stone, and none
where she used to weep tears.
The burned-out ravine
is serene.

She Goes to War

Her face is her enemy.
She does battle in the mirror. Look!
This scar dates from Heidelberg,
that one from Saturday night.

There was a Polish boy, son of the ambassador
to Brazil, who carried a sword on the train.
All day long rain broke against the glass
and ran under the track, pooling between ties.

Back home, she lies in bed, scant sun shining
through eucalyptus leaves. Look here,
the deadliest confrontation is the one fought under cover
of camouflage, foliage

stenciled over the breast,
twigs and berries sprouting among the tangled strands
of hair she can do nothing with.
There is a man with a gun and he empties it into her chest.

The Pines Without Peer

The pines without peer
Are taller than air.

They grow in the sky,
Their roots in your eye.

And the tops of the pines wave
From the top of the sky, brave

As banners. And the tops
Of the pines are steps

To the high, wheeling
Stars. And your brain is reeling

And the trees are falling,
And you are falling

In a forest, pulled,
Drawn, blinded and mauled,

And you are the ground
And the wound

And the one wild sound.

Fission

I

The atoms buzz like bees,
Splendiferously. Trees
Spring into leaf and light
Kisses night good-bye.

II

Here's rain and grassblade!
Made for each other—
I seem to see you in shade
And sun, the trickiest weather.

III

A solitary fly
Sews the sky around my head,
Stitching with invisible thread.
Time is this needle's eye.

IV

You lie, you lie.
I unstopper my veins and drink
My heart dry.
Call me Alice. I shrink.

V

I split. I spin through space at full
Tilt, keel, careen, smash, and mushroom
Into smoke beside your oaken heart.
Death does us part.

IV

As for man, his days are as grass:
   as a flower of the field, so he
   flourisheth.
For the wind passeth over it, and
   it is gone; and the place thereof
   shall know it no more.

—Psalms 103:15–16

For Teen-Age Boys Murdered in Texas:
The Refusal to Dramatize Bloodlust

This once we will vanquish violence,
stake the heart & cross
the spirit's path

so it won't rise, that godawful
gorge hot & grainy
moving against the constricted throat

This once we will forgo
theater (that's
tribute from a poet,

ask Dickey or Bly)
I tell you
27 children is reason enough

to burn certain books,
go outside,
see how the sky looks

when day breaks thru
O creeping mist of the midnight unspeakable, lie
still upon the lilies & dissolve

The Fate of the Children

Abraham reads the entrails of the ram and foretells the future.

Lately, in Cambodia, they tear the children apart.
What Solomon only threatened, they make real.
One soldier grabs an arm,
another a leg.

Meanwhile, in Czechoslovakia,
the children are prevented from living with their parents,
     refugees.
Reunification of this family is "in contradiction with the
     interests of the socialist state."

In Russia, little girls wear white bows in their hair;
gauze butterflies perch on their blonde or brunette curls.
If their parents object to the lack of civil liberty, or, say,
     simply to the sudden disappearance of a dear friend,
the little girls pay for their fathers' "sins."
(And the fathers pay also, and the mothers.)
The little girls are pinned to their places like butterflies
     in glass cases.

Then again, according to eyewitnesses,
Lieutenant Calley tore an infant from the arms of a Buddhist
     priest,
tossing it into the air like a clay pigeon,
and shot it forever dead with his army-issue M-16.

None of this is poetry; it is fact.
And not only fact, but act.
And not only act, but raw fat and warm blood, hope expiring
like breath, and shadow
beating a menacing tattoo on the wall of the house in a high
     wind, like an overgrown bush,
and I refuse to pretend it is poetry,
seeing it is not even food.
Lord, Lord . . . what is poetic about the way we slaughter our
     children,
the way we sacrifice our sons
like lambs,
yes, precisely: like lambs?

Snapshot, 1945

The Butterfly Boy, Private First Class, flies, flits
From bar to bar, glancing upon the flowers
Of Tokyo; and when he's old he sits
By his small fire, robbing dreams from the crushed hours.

My Mother's Father

lived in a sawmill, whittling
houses for strangers.
On Sunday he rowed to church
via bayou backwaters. All his daughters
dreamed of Ahab and Ulysses
(they were at that age).
They drifted like leaves pried from the riverbank.
Their bare limbs glowed in the late of day.
When twilight came, the woody cypress grew
shadows, and fairy rings
sprang up and disappeared
overnight.

On Receiving the News of a Friend's
Father's Death, at Four A.M.

You rise out of deep sleep
like a tree out of earth,
slowly; nothing seems worth
this radical, forced leap

into consciousness. Air
encloses you, opens
your throat—the invisible physician listens,
is always listening, to your heart beating there,

at the base of your throat.
You are thinking, Worry.
It's the one word caught
in your leafy brain. You're sorry

even before the fact; then the telephone
goes off, loud as a shot.
We live dimly, under the earth, but
die awake, above and alone.

Baby Friedman,

grow fat on your father's grin
& someday let your mother know you're glad
she said yes & let him in

Sharks

". . . [A]ll angel is not'ing more dan de shark
well goberned.'"
                    —Perth in *Moby-Dick*

You have to keep them under close watch.
They attack without warning, sudden as a squall,
underslung jaws swinging loose on the gilled latch

like a baby getting ready to bawl
its head off. Treading time, they circle the sole
survivor, never doubting he'll fall

from grace soon enough, dizzied by their sunlit shoal.
Light yaws and tacks, blown back against his battered vision
by the wind their fins wake. Whole

days drift by, like seaweed. Though history seems to shun
him, and sunburn raises blisters on his mouth,
he sucks salt from the Pacific Ocean

as a baby pulls a breast. Sharks swim south
of Paradise, around the Cape of Sin,
but he who clings like a barnacle to the lessons of his youth

earns the salute of a scaly fin.
He may yet teach a school of hammerheads
to dance on the head of a pin.

Going Down on America: The Regional Poet

Turned on to the transcendent, he holds her
in his arms, strokes her sunny hair.
Such sweet skin is coming into view
as the clothes of Straight are shed
over New Jersey & kicked aside
into the wide Missouri River—

He pledges allegiance to lightfilled breasts,
to the drops of shine spilled
on Shenandoah's applerich harvest.

In this union of smoke & suck he enters a state just west
of grace where Wyoming is what cowboys do
on Saturday night when the boss has paid them up
& the wind smells of Montana carried downstream,
clean but unmistakable.

O Mount Rushmore,
move him to your eye of stone!

In wheat fields he may dream
of stalks of sun,

discover blue shadows
in the shingles of the fallen pinecone!

The seventh day dawns somewhere above the fabulous Sierras
& in a whirlwind of contradiction funnels itself south
into the dusk of his throat,
enlightens his heart,
& sets the flesh to dancing upon bare bones
across known borders
into a land lost
to reality.

Five Views of an Artist

1. *The Bright-limbed Man*

He is a lost art:
the techniques of his existence
have faded into antiquity

like paint on a weathered wall.
I no longer remember
pose or perspective or what

distinguishes him from all
the figures in the past—
beyond being last.

Perhaps someday scholars will resurrect
love and restore its colors
to my memory,

and the bright-limbed man will step animatedly
down from his mural
into bedewed and overgrown grass.

2. *The Man of Fertile Reflection*

Moonlight falls, like a mulch of old leaves,
on his head, while deep inside the skull
radiance puts down roots

and sends forth shoots.
When he enters my house
he brings the brightness of autumn

into my arms, and holding him,
I lean on light
like a dreamer on bark,

growing against the dark.
He is the thrill of brilliance, the fruitful and illuminating thought.
All night I lie among his limbs

while the cold wind climbs
up from the sea. He grows tired
of me. Suddenly it's dawn—

he's gone.

3. *Loving the Man Who Absorbs Substance*

He is the man who absorbs substance
from shadow and seems
to thrive on the gray

matter of my mind, doubt and despair,
the ridicule of dreams.
He is eating my heart out!

I stew in my own vital juices
until the marrow of my backbone streams
with the consistency of wet-running clay

into his hungry hands.
My colorless lack of definition teams
with his artistic appetite

to make us one,
increase of shade consuming sun.
When I'm dark, he's done.

4. *Man in His Image*

Chiaroscuro contains him.
If he moves, it is within this prodigal garden
of light and absence

where the one tree grows that will dispense
a taste of the true vision.
Such shrubbery blinds me.

Morning finds me
dazzled, ravenous and blue, crunching thorns
between my teeth. He is hidden

among wind-blown branches, forbidden
to reveal himself to my brazen gaze into
that holy orchard, lest sight astonish me

beyond belief to the point where sheer satiation must admonish me
against a stigmatism of the soul,
miserable spotted spoilage! Is he the unplucked mote in my eye?

Or am I?

5. *The Disappearing Man*

When no one is watching, I pile up ripe maize and turnips
in my skirt and steal past my metrical clothesline.
Dew shocks thin-skinned soles

rushing in where angels. This is virgin territory,
stripped to the essential shape, plain and full of wood,
her damp air drying out

as day approaches. In this clearing, I kneel
beside an emblematic totem bearing
the countless sweet, first fruits of creation, clawed

into being by a bird of perilous beauty
whose webbed wings, like sin, span the world from prehistory
to the present. But its beak's been broken in.

My harvest is for the man
who saddles the wind and rides out of sight.
Light labors long into the night.

Marshaling a First Line of Defense
Against the Great Hunter

Old Taurus,
                    transfixed by Orion's shield,
lower your head and charge!
                              The sisters sing,
and cling to the hairy tufts on your hide.
                                        Turning
from side to side under the horns, Aldebaran,
concentrated, crazed, fanatic eye,
scouts the hunter in the winter sky
who tracks your stars' spoor.
                              You snort and paw
the air, and your hooves trample my hair into mud.

Scorpion,
              I saw the sun on your back
when you dropped down the crack between the front porch steps
into cool earth, swift as Mercury.
                                   *
                              Later,
I married your sting.
                    Time chastises the confident woman,
making her kiss mere air.
                         *
                    O Silver, my zodiac star,
hero, avenger, shining arachnid, come
once more from the south in my gloomy season.
Clamp your claws on cruel Orion.

Twitchy-nosed Nibbler
                    with long ears,
don't tremble. Fear fluffs your faint stars
into view, and your foolish tail's a puff of sparkling space.
The smallest creature has its right to a place in the Great Chain
of Light. We'll see to it that no one snuffs you out or switches you
off.
          But if Orion should spot you where you crouch, spring
out of sight,
                    hop over the horizon,
                                        and feed on bright sky
above faraway Siberia.
                    There,
you will be free to multiply the planets beyond measure.
Sterile as the moon, I'll take rare pleasure in your newborn bunnies;
they'll be the children I never had, little constellations
to stroke and pet.

Sneak Scraps to Sirius,
                    throw him off
the scent. Tongue thick with grease,
he pants in my face. I endure
every humiliation.
                    *
          Procyon runs ahead.
I call him back to my bed, and when
this lecherous old world laughs at me,
I play dead.
          *
          That mean man's most loyal companions
I will seduce from his side, the dog stars and insanity.

Orion's Lion's Skin
                    drops, netting
me. I am his last catch,
after the friends, the husbands, have fallen away,
after intention's flesh is realized as actual decay.
The dogs had their day; it was night.
                              I gobble earth's air,
fleeting, and my toes bite into loam, like teeth.
                              His shin winks.
Supremely careless, the great man spills Betelgeuse
down the front of his sky.
                    I leap as high
as any flood tide, butting my head
against shield and sword's broadside, club and cat hide.
                              I can't
breathe, can't run. He throws me over
his shoulder like a sack. Everything's black.
When the sun comes up, I'm stiff
as a corpse inside my skin,
                    cold as the dew on my chin,
                              no longer
one who stands between the hunter and you.

V

What thou seest, write in a book. . . .

—Revelation 1:11

A Bird's-Eye View of Einstein

You start from the point of perch.
                                       Here, air's restless
And lambent, licking at leaves like candlelight.
Next, you hold your candle high.
                                    Looking off,
You will be able to see a century
Of holocausts, smoking on the lip of space.
Go ahead and preen: Before we sing or swing,
We start from point of view.
                              Time, that flies, lights
On the optic nerve and beats its wings against
My brain. My skull's a nest socked between branch
And sky. I train my eagle eye on dark
Shadows scudding across the hemisphere.
I swoop; I lift; shadows are preyed on here.
The crop of time is choked with sigh and tear.

Concerning the First Relation: Bridegroom

Last, you listen. One cry echoes, echoes,
And echoes. It's insistent as sleet but light
As light. The skyline bats it back and forth.
Like a shuttlecock slapped out of season,
It maps a parabolic flight, and fall.
I track its arc, am cautioned, turn away,
Trim my lamp.
                       I go down before I go
Down. The hotel sign spills neon on the street
And neon stains the snow. My husband stands
With his back to the window, looking in.
His hands rest on my head, my hair towels
The snowflakes from his feet, and if I sin,
I sip salvation like sweet wine, wiping
My mouth on his thigh.
                          Still, unquiet shadows
Ring the room, and remind me of someone
Who stalks my steps down dead-end streets and stops
If I stop and waits, patient and intent,
While I climb the stairs, use the phone, undress,
And drop off into unprotected sleep.
When the light goes out, I marry the man
Who ties my tongue, dazzles my brain, and turns

My wrists to water. He meets me under the roof
Of my mouth, where I leak profanity and store
Desire against the day of reckoning
When our hearts go hungry.
                    I eat the Christ.
My face grows warm with work. I feel foolish
As a virgin: My spine's exposed to cold
Air and my scalp smells of sweat. I could swear
He mocks my greed and the servility
It brings me to, but spares me, from a sense
Of pity or proportion, or because
He's got better things to do than scorn
Venus for her visibility, earth
For being walked on. Forbearance makes me sick
With shame.
           Aquila's Altair shies from sight,
But I run out into the night, spewing
This holy seed upon the waste land.
                        O
Men and women, love according to law.
The one you covenanted with is jealous
Of your affections, and causes the child
Of adultery to curse the day he was born.
Divorce yourselves from idols. Raise your young
On the fruits of faith.
                I weep bitterly,
Scavenging in back alleys for flyspecked scraps
And moldy crusts. I lean against the tree
That glows green-black, with a bark like opal,
Under the street lamp. Moral knowledge sucks
Up moisture from the soil of paradise.
How many trees history exacts, and how
Broken the land becomes!
                 I rake kindling
From my unclean hair.
             Then the sun, burning
Up an Eddic vine, tops out, flaring up
In a brief explosion of photosynthesis
Manqué, the pinnate green gone awry, white
Hot and flashy like a tree of mirrors,
The golden bough issuing in crystal light.
At this point Phlegethon purls and spurtles

Beneath Boulevard Bridge, and overflows
The Fan, inflaming whole families with thirst
For the inconceivable. A monstrous
Appetite, glutting itself on human flesh
Gutted by fire, hankers after that still
Tougher substance speared on a stick of wood,
And seared by this savage culture.

                                    All myths
Meet and mingle here, weep, giggle and come
Sour as pulp in my mouth. Nothing is born
That dies. My mouth will hatch a skyful of
Raucous words that endure endlessly, like
Certain sound waves, retrievable, static
And irrelevant.

                        And once in Richmond
When Monument was buried under snow,
And even the General's horse seemed hewn from blue
Ice, I saw my best beloved, He of
The Black Moods, reel in his steaming breath, gulp
The windy words, grow fat and gouty, lie
Swollen beneath the slush and drift, waiting,
Helpless as an infant, for warm weather
And release from earth. Then I nailed him down
Upon that visionary rock, and sowed
Bird seed in his wounds. The gashes yielded
A fowl harvest, an ornithology
Of blood, and feathers flowered in his veins
Until he suffocated by the force
Of that green fuse that lit the landscape up
By day, and burned it out by night.

                                    I watch
Disaster feeding on the crumbs of stale
Hope. She grows up, grows fat, grows old and dies.
An eyrie cheeping crashes on the scree,
Like surf. Nestlings persist. Her fluids clot
Their down, while maggots breed in bloodied straw.
Each hungry beak will raid its brother's craw.

Concerning the Middle Term: Ghost

My brother lives in Bronxville, Belsen, Rome,
Belfast and Quebec. He has three blind wives
Who wind the clock on Sunday. See how they

Run: one to Reno, one to Richie Small.
But one's got something cooking in the oven
And it's not by Pillsbury.
                              I recall
The names and dates he wishes I'd forget.
How, feeling up my friend from school, he jabbed
His hand on a strategic safety pin;
The woman from Haiti whose hair came off in his hand
One night; and the night we said our name over
And over, while the cigarette between
His fingers smouldered and went out, and light
Held its breath an hour or two and then blew
Out the day.
                    We lay on the outer shore
Of space, cast up by a soundless solar
Wind from the depths of time. Each light wave touched
His hair with damp; I dried him with my breath.
But we grow old and grow apart. Betray
Thy brother: This is the first death. My heart
Collects vibrations like a shell, tuning
The stars' breeze to a fever pitch, and still,
When wives walk slowly round the universe
And spin the orbit of our planet out
According to their measure, I deny
I ever knew him.
                        I play hide-and-seek
In Ithaca. My brother combs the gorge.
I am seven. I wear my birthstone, pack
A pistol, and I hug my quick shadow
In secret, but my brother finds me out
Behind the evergreen.
                            Is this the tree
In Revelation 22, verse two,
Whose leaves restore the nations, and, if not,
Why did my brother carve his name and mine
In a Cupid's target, and why was this
Woody scroll unrolled in darkness, and read
Among the dying and the dead? Something
Keeps me, and keeps me looking for that lost
Word, the one which answers to the grave.
                                                    O
Bereft and saddened populations, be
Gladdened by light, and channel light downward

To earth, and let it wash the flesh away
From these dry bones, that the hand of the Lord
May gentle them, and move the slow marrow
To praise and a beginning.
                              When we raise
Our eyes and fling them out like stones, rippling
The surface of the Milky Way, we look
Backward in time. My brother used to dive
For motes. They float among the atoms, scarce
As pearls, and each pearl plucked will buy the eye
Of a needle. Then he drowned. And now I skim
Galactic shallows, looking for the one
Husband of my sightless sisters. I glide
Along the currents of Andromeda,
Because my brother's body, unfathomed
For two million years, preceding Perseus,
Lies broken on the reef, locked in a cold
Luminescence.
                    I see the whitened bones,
Scoured as though by salt, drifting aimlessly
Like driftwood, from world to world in an ocean
Of light. What nebula, what nebula
Irrigates the shrubs of heaven!
                                      At this
Point Phlegethon charts a new course, cresting
On a hillside outside home. I feed fish
Of fire to orphans. Still they beg for more.
Give them more: This was my brother's body,
With which he warmed my own. All night we crouched
Side by side, holding hands, while bombs splintered
The sky into slivers of light, and one
Spark lodged deep in his windpipe, fatal as
An arrow dipped in venom, and I sucked
The poison out, but silence told me he
Was gone away, wedded to the woman
I was not.
                I see disaster brooding
Over the past. Her wide and nervous wings
Eclipse the echoing moon, but soon the sun
Startles her into flight. Not until night
Does she return, bringing burning and old
Mad grief for the fatherless and unborn.

Part Three: Infinity

Our father moves among his many rooms.
Silent as light, he builds and blueprints, both
At once, in the single act of passing
Through. His house is walled with light. The window
Gives onto a lawn of light stretching in all
Directions back onto itself. I find
My view encompassed by my pupil, shrunk
Before the fact of brilliance. My tongue's gone dry
As dry ice, and my hands sweat salt water
Streams. There is a taste of ash on my teeth.
The half-moon of my thumbnail shows its dark
Side to the sun, and hangs in the branches of
My body. My blood glows, and flows uphill—
And still I'm circumscribed by being, fenced
In by myself. My father locks the door
And throws the key away.
                              Here is the room
Where the music is made.
                              Here is the room
Where violins are played, and light is made
Of light, and sound falls to the ground like fruit
Shaken from a full tree.
                              Here is the room
Where sound is splayed into chromatic scales.
Here is the room where violins are played.
I listen on my back; my father counts
The measured rests strewn freely and with glee
Down the page, like centers of gravity,
Equilibrating energy.
                              I am
That discordant note which calls attention
To itself. My soul fidgets and rasps. I cough.
My creating father doesn't care how
Tightly music clasps my hand, how violent
Are the strokes his rosined bow has drawn across
My neck, nor what lesser pulse keeps time there,
Nor does he hear how wonderfully well I wail
In harmony.
                    I skulk in corners crammed
With old resentment. I chew sugar cane
In Baton Rouge, and I search the scorched fields

For my father, but he lies hidden in
The earth, asleep and dreaming of the day
When sunlight sloshing on his face will wake
Him up to play duets with Einstein.
His artful innocence has undone mine.
If I find him, I'll flush him out and plant
Cold kisses on his forehead for a sign.
The cross I work to snare him with is made
Of peat moss, and it smells of bitter smoke.
I lurk behind the blind and bring down birds
Of peace. Such small and airy skeletons
Sizzle in the Lake of Fire, and sink!
                                        O
Children of judgment, choose goodness. Banish
Arbitrary hurt, but know that the root
Wrenched from dry ground weeps gravel and requires
Righting, or all the oppressed land will groan
Under blanching stocks and sharp, sunburned rocks
Will bruise and singe your soles.
                                My father slips
Through tall sweetness.
                                Instantly, Phlegethon
Leaps to the surface, spilling drops of flame
On Golgotha. Someone dozes on the bank
And baits his line from a can of skulls, fishing
For martyrs. I reel in my breath, and steal
Past poetry, to where my father waits
With sad expectancy in his eyes; I think
He knows how much he wronged me when he went
Away, but I am as implacable
As death, and just as difficult to please.
I strap him down upon the cross and skew
His skinned knees skyward. I lap lightstruck nails
Under my tongue, and spit them out one by
One. My hammer drives holes into the hands
That never touched me but only ideal
And melody, and I caress the knobs
Of his ankles, before I splice the flesh.
I soothe the tensing veins with vinegar.
I give him vinegar to drink, and sponge his brow
With vinegar, and now darkness slams down
Over the earth, like space foreclosing on

Itself, and ominous comets contract
To points without dimension, swallowing
Their toxic streams, and stars are pinched out in
That split second between dread and despair
When we become aware of God, and know
That he is absent. Thunder claps our dumb
Eyes shut, and lashes the lids with hailstones,
And earthquake heaves stony tombs up like puke.
Cry woe.
        I will split his side in two.
                                  Blood
Explodes.
        I will wreak vengeance on the one
Who refused my sex.
                   Cry woe.
                        I will blast
Him like an atom bomb, and crawl into
The crater of his corpse. Lymph and mucus
Are contaminated.
                Cry woe.
                    I crawl
Into the hollow in his side, and place
My head against his heart. As unresponsive
As a desert to the changing seasons,
He suffers my cheek. When I whisper, no one
Replies, and nothing blinks or sighs or moves,
Except the wind, worming its way through bone
And carrion.
            Down all the blown chambers
Of his ruining body, my cry echoes:
Why hast thou forsaken me?
                  Disaster
Picks the brainpan clean. Memory spatters
Darksome plumage, imagination sticks
In the flexed craw, and sense is vexed by sense.
Now is the hour. Now is the hour of woe.
I will flood the forbidden zone with tears
And rain tears on his viscera, and tears

Will run in his veins, pooling among the parched
Platelets.
              The trunk takes root.
                                   The shot limbs stir,
And light and sound swell and ripen like small
Round mustard seeds which grow into the kingdom
Of heaven, and bear faith.
                        Birds of the air
Stuff their nests with sinew, and make their nests
In the drafty sockets.
                  Now is the hour
Of closure.
             Now is the hour of reprise.
                            Now is
The hour of recapitulation.
                  Time
Sings in the tree.